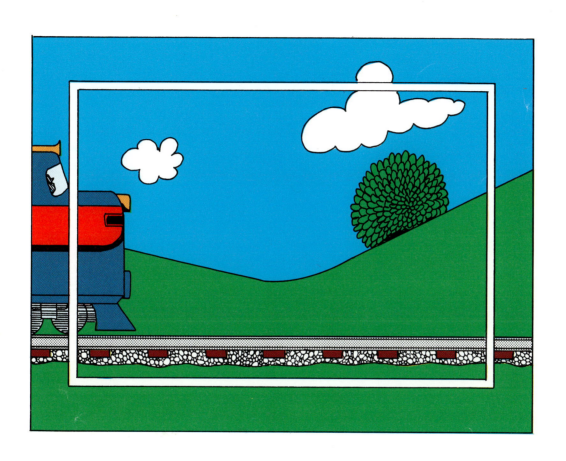

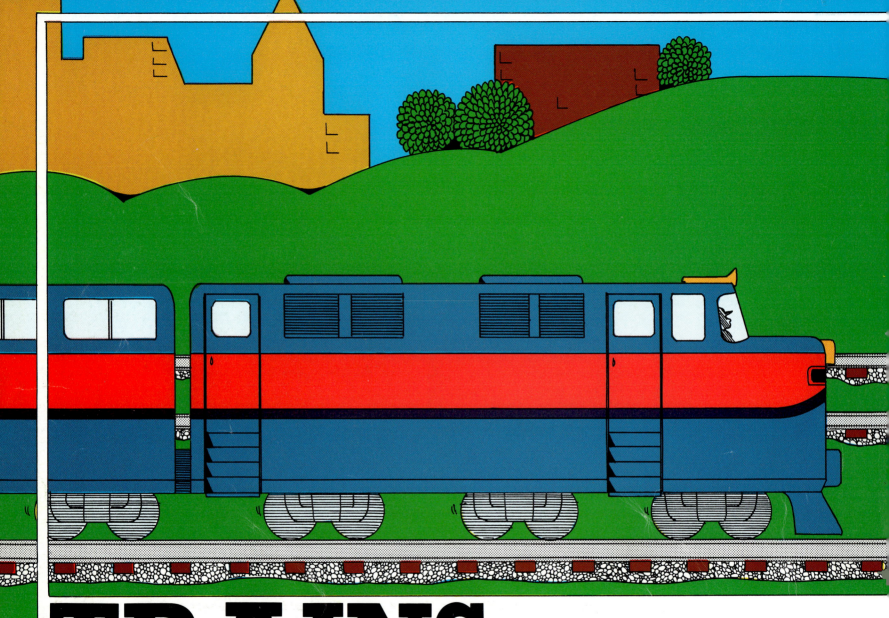

TRAINS

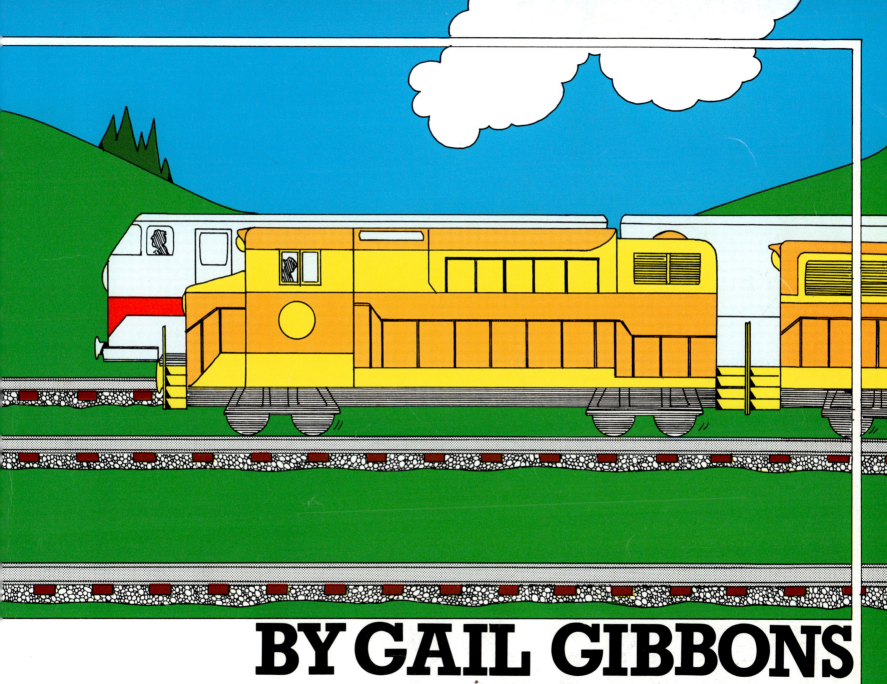

BY GAIL GIBBONS

HOLIDAY HOUSE · NEW YORK

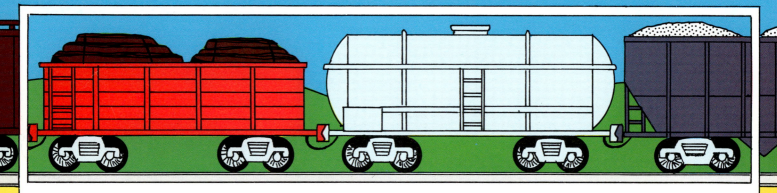

**Special thanks to William E. Faughnan of the Boston & Maine Railroad
and
John F. McLeod of Amtrak (The National Railroad Passenger Corporation)**

Copyright © 1987 by Gail Gibbons
All rights reserved
Printed in the United States of America

Library of Congress Cataloging-in-Publication Data

Gibbons, Gail.
Trains.

Summary: Examines different kinds of trains, past
and present, describing their features and functions.
1. Railroads—Juvenile literature.   [1. Railroads—
Trains]   I. Title.
TF148.G53   1987   625.1   86-19595
ISBN 0-8234-0640-7
ISBN 0-8234-0699-7 (pbk.)

Many kinds of trains move along the tracks . . .

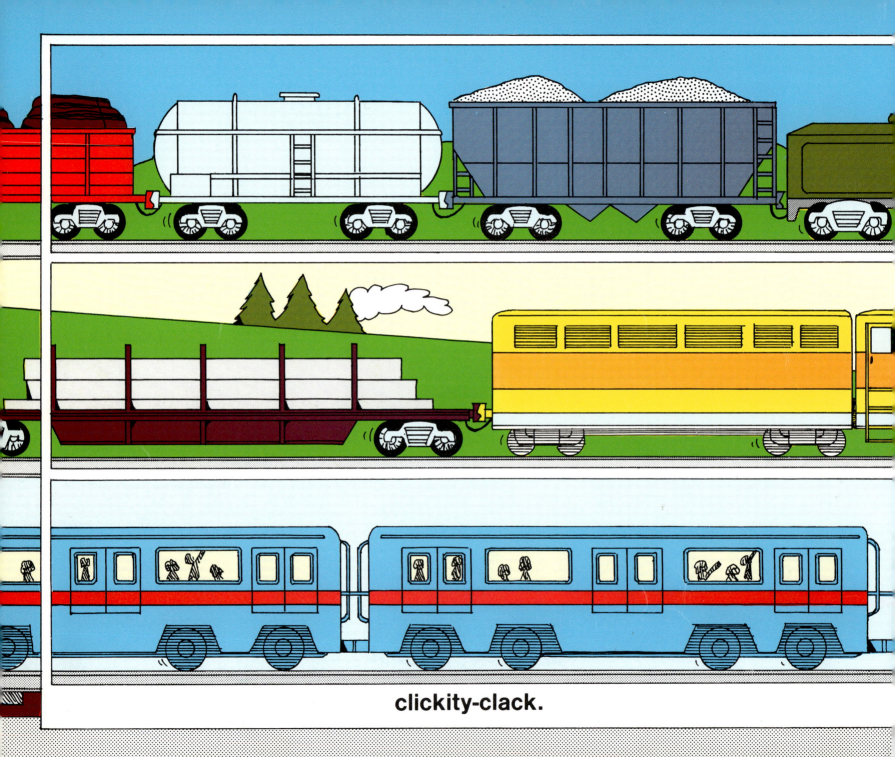

clickity-clack.

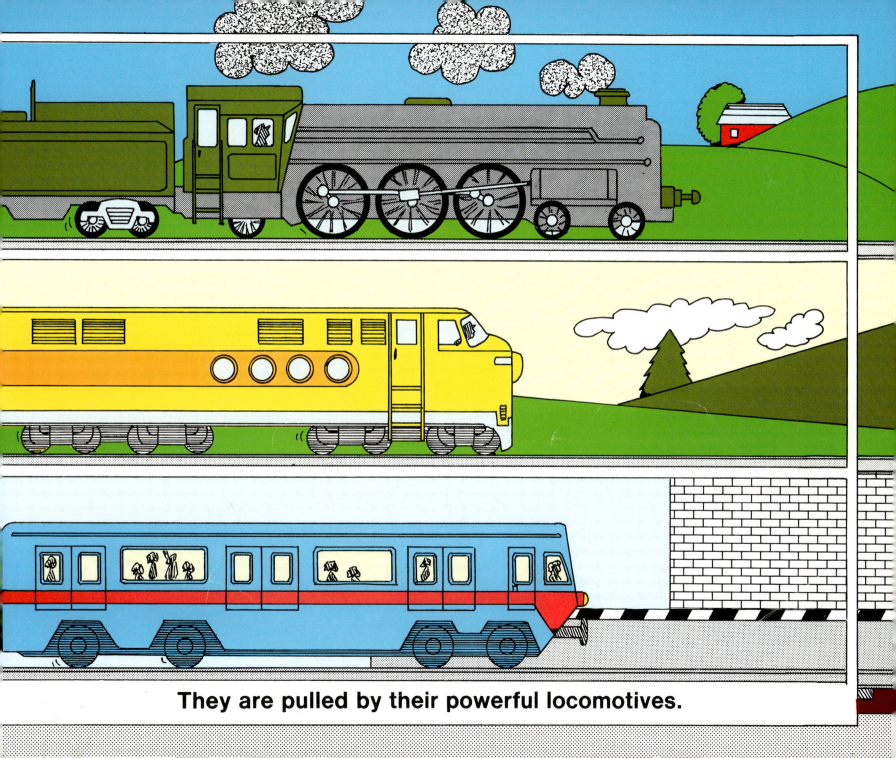

They are pulled by their powerful locomotives.

The first locomotives were built about 150 years ago.

fireman

engineer

steam engine

The trains were pulled by steam engines.
They used wood or coal for fuel.

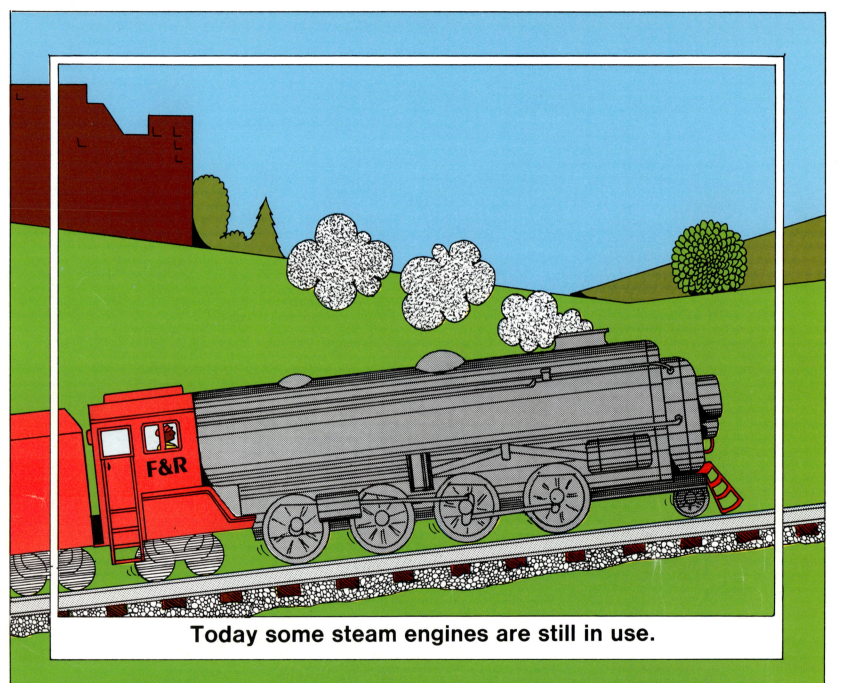

Today some steam engines are still in use.

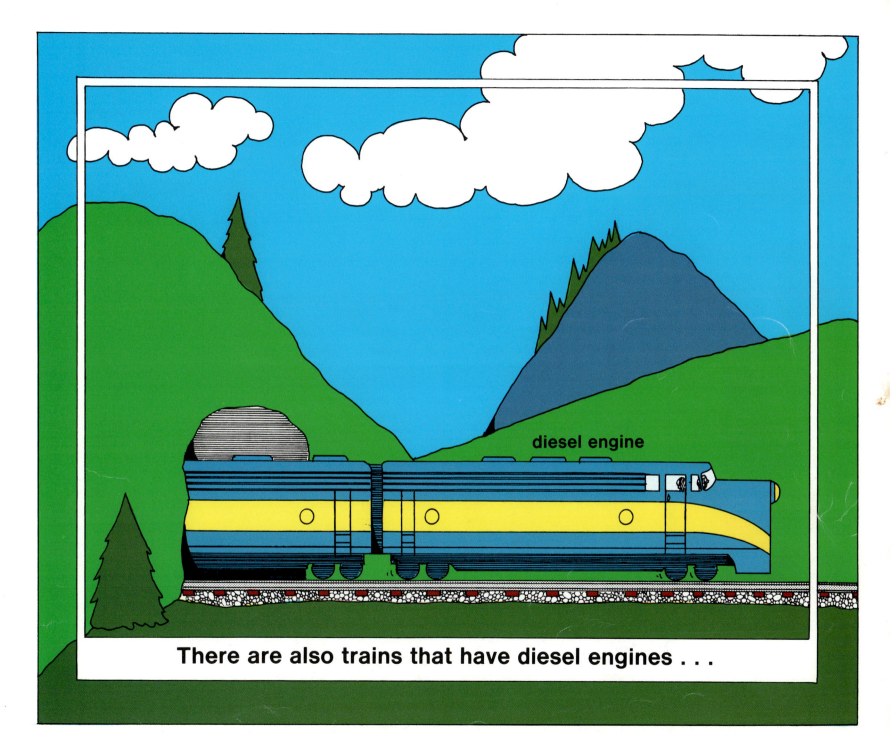

diesel engine

There are also trains that have diesel engines . . .

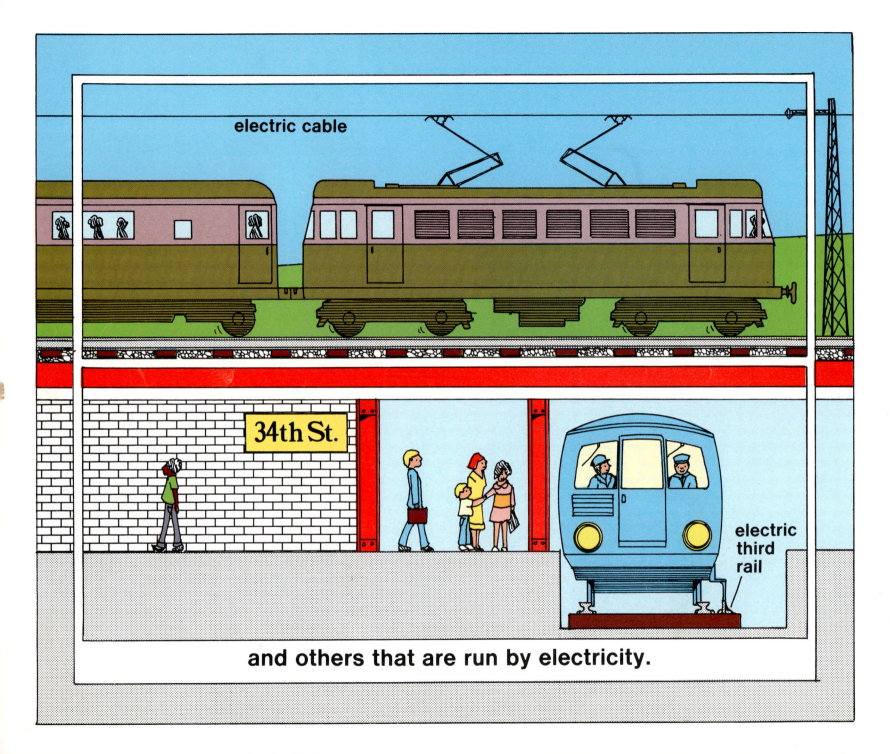

electric cable

34th St.

electric
third
rail

and others that are run by electricity.

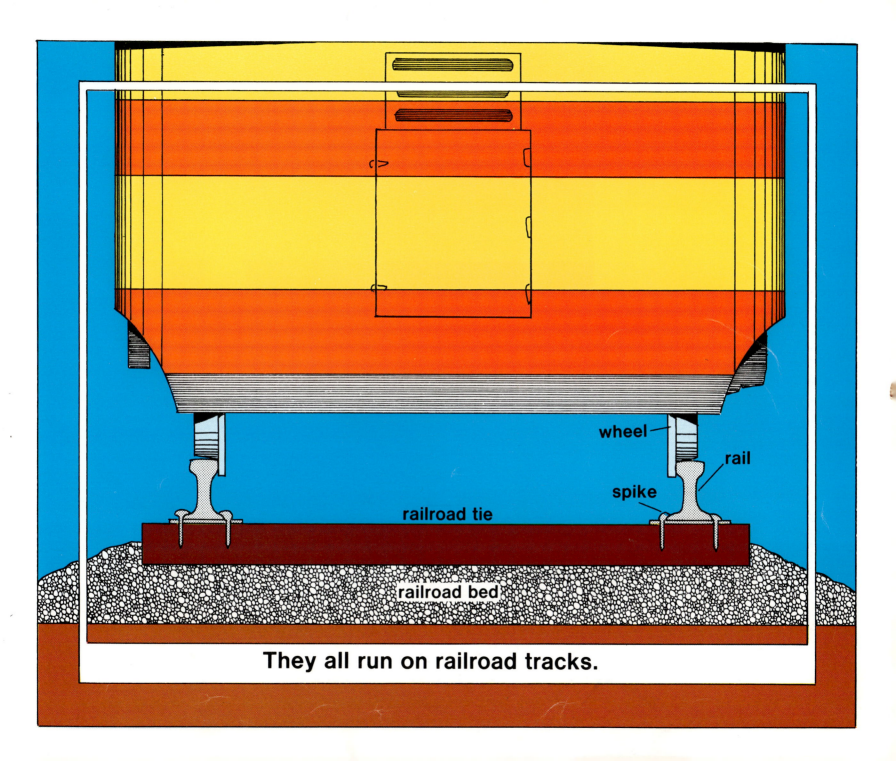

wheel

rail

spike

railroad tie

railroad bed

They all run on railroad tracks.

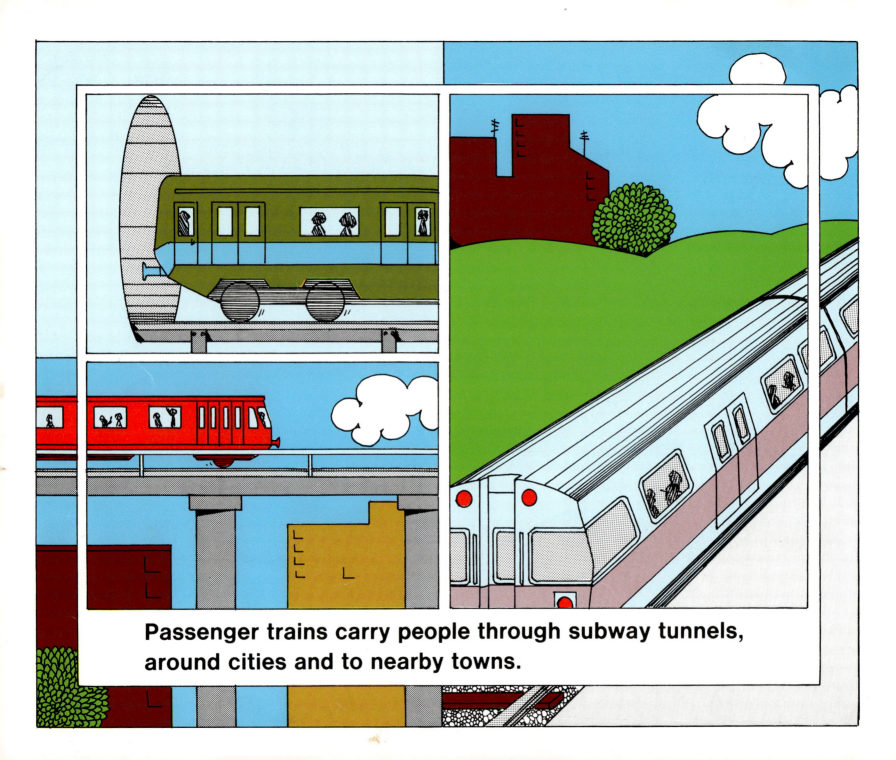

Passenger trains carry people through subway tunnels, around cities and to nearby towns.

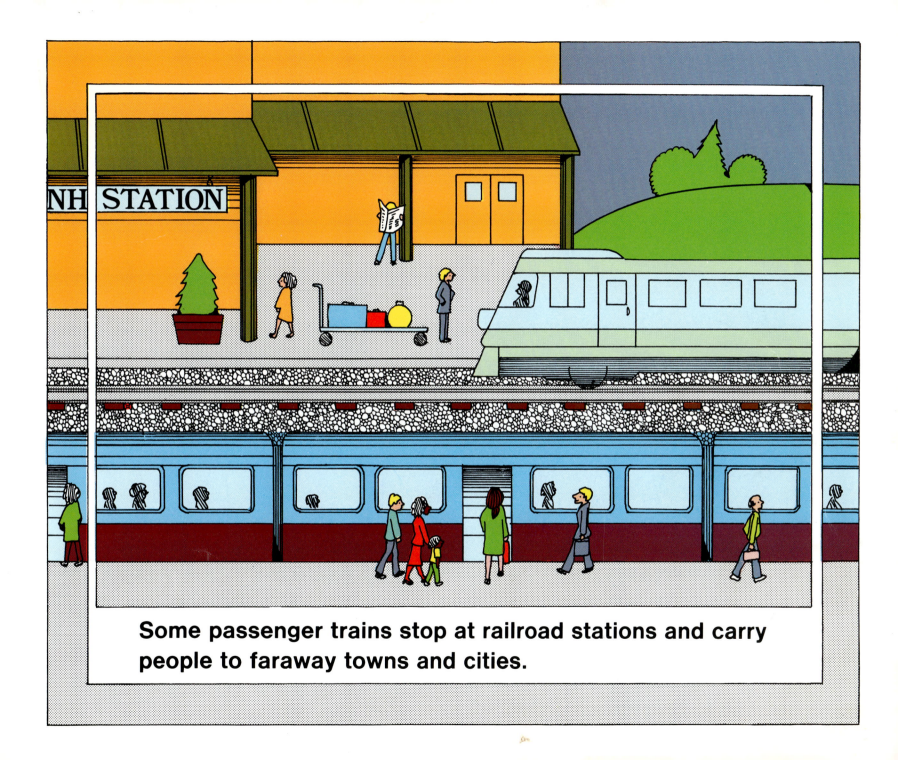

Some passenger trains stop at railroad stations and carry people to faraway towns and cities.

dining car

Passengers can eat . . .

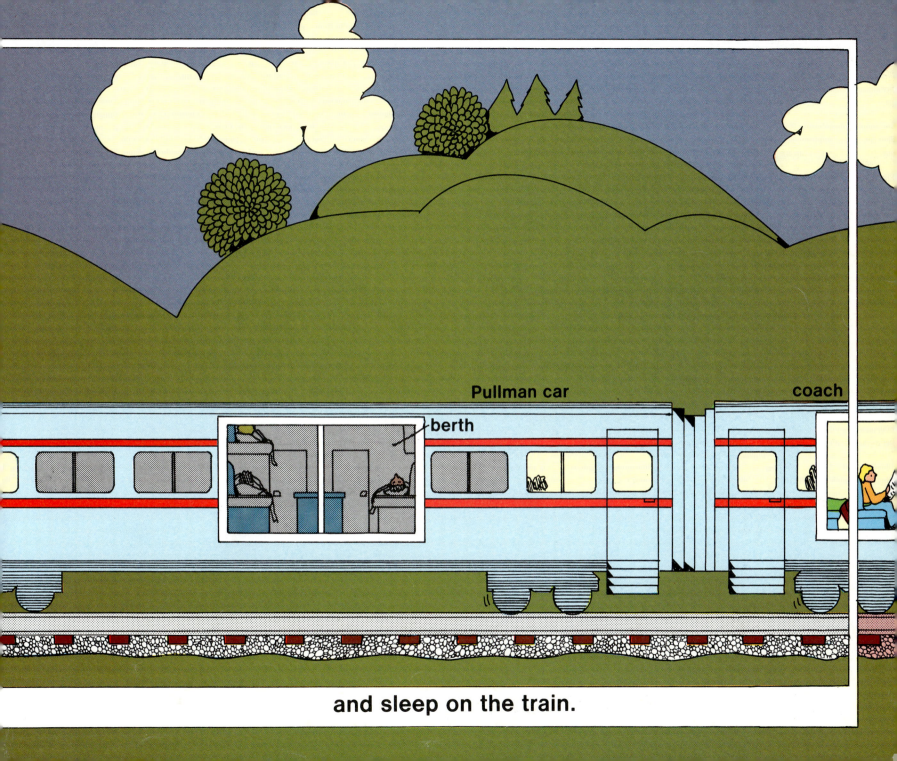

Pullman car

coach

berth

and sleep on the train.

There are freight trains, too. They carry heavy loads.

Sometimes more than one engine is needed to pull a very long train.

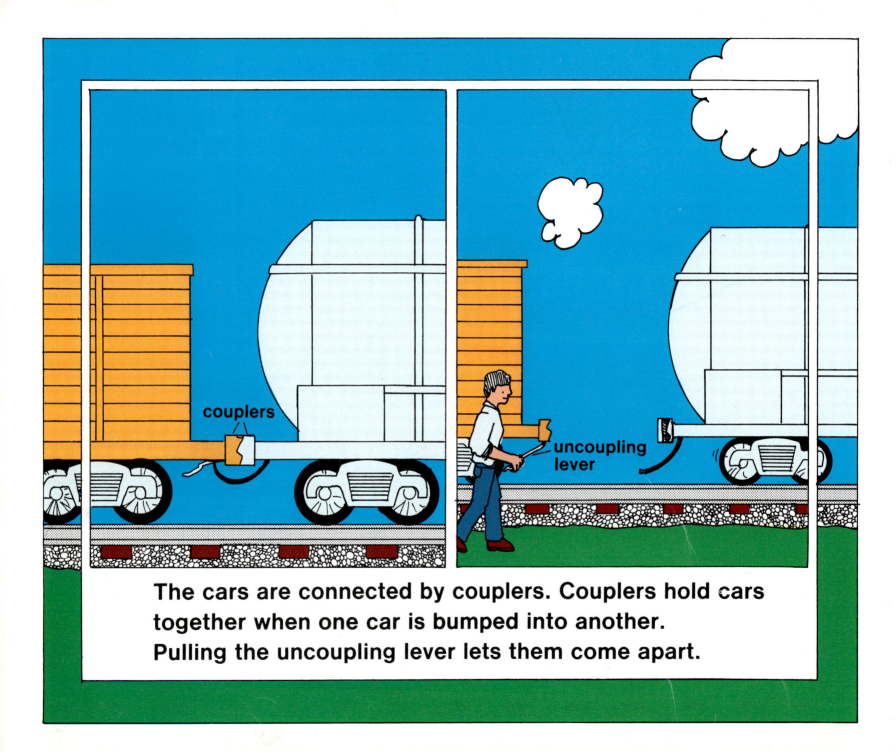

couplers

uncoupling lever

The cars are connected by couplers. Couplers hold cars together when one car is bumped into another.
Pulling the uncoupling lever lets them come apart.

Freight trains have lots of different cars.
Flatcars haul many kinds of cargo.

Refrigerator cars carry food that needs to be kept fresh.

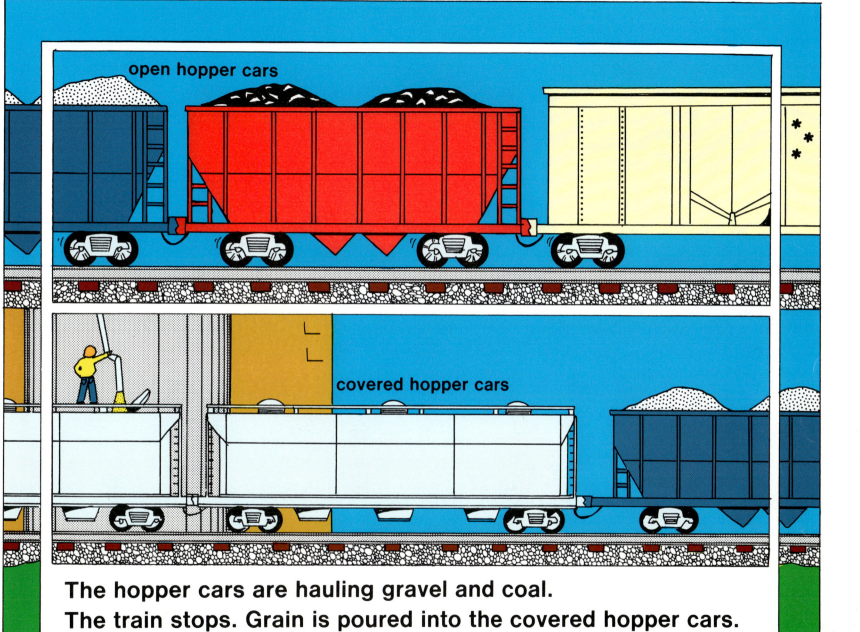

open hopper cars

covered hopper cars

The hopper cars are hauling gravel and coal.
The train stops. Grain is poured into the covered hopper cars.

The train moves on. Piggyback cars carry truck trailers.

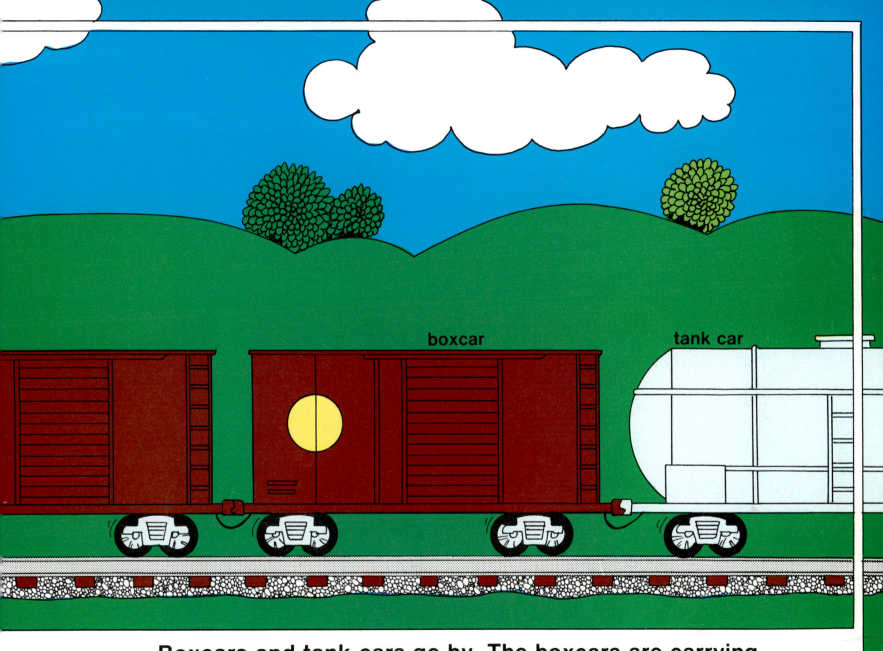

boxcar

tank car

Boxcars and tank cars go by. The boxcars are carrying furniture. The tank cars are carrying oil.

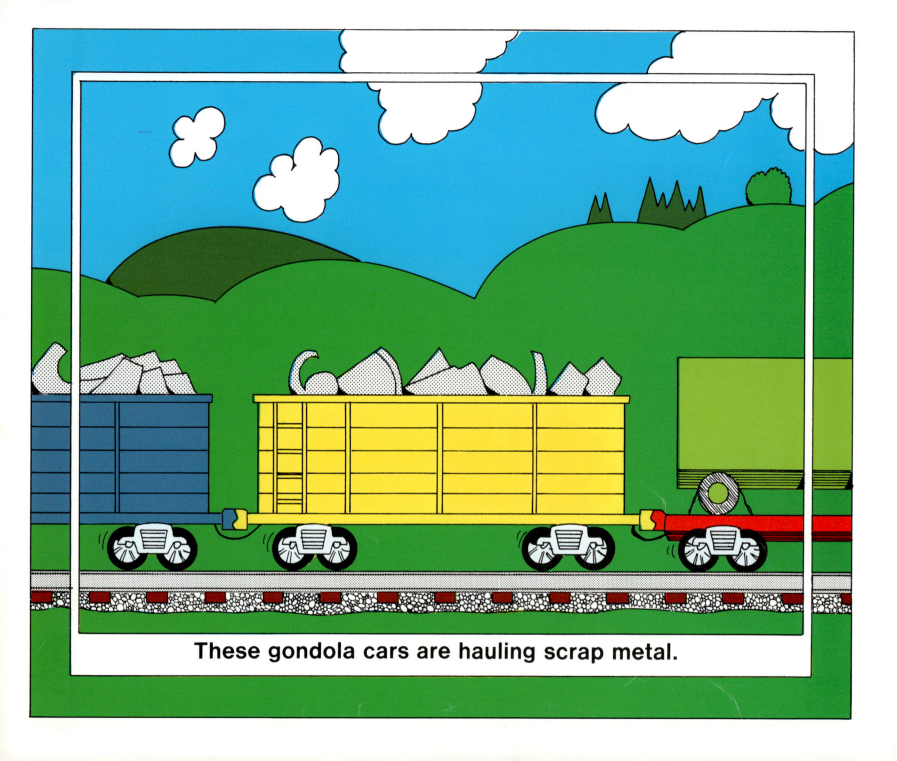

These gondola cars are hauling scrap metal.

The train stops. Grain is dumped from the covered hopper cars.

The train moves on again. Three-level rack cars roll by carrying shiny new cars. At the end of the train is . . .

the caboose. The caboose is for the train crew.

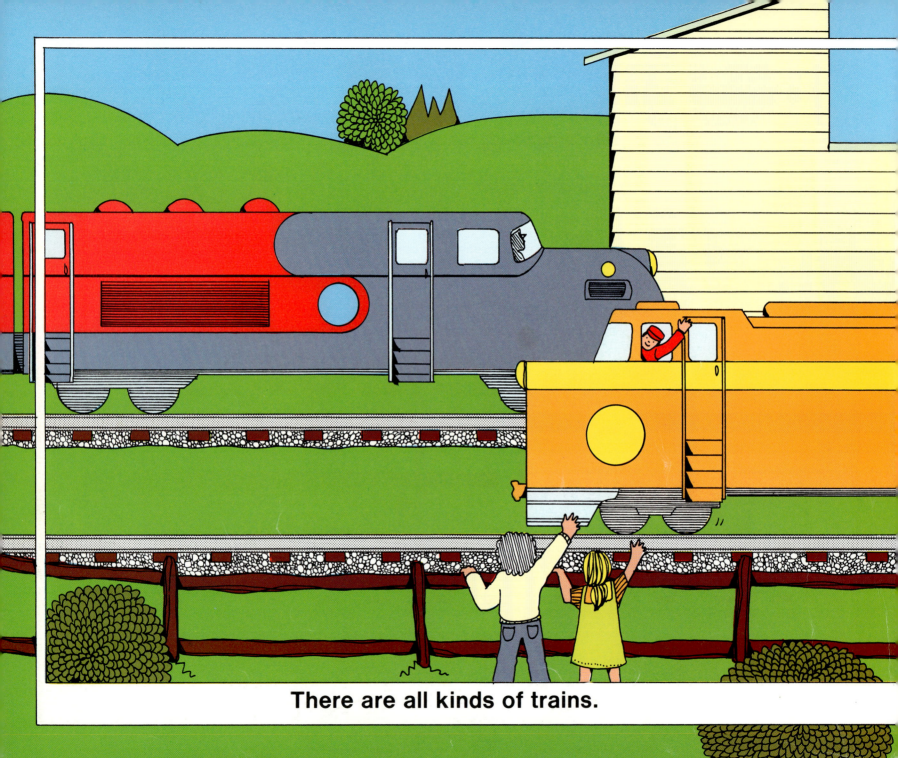

There are all kinds of trains.

It is fun to watch them go by.

SIGNS & SIGNALS

Some are for people driving cars or walking.

Railroad crossing ahead

Railroad crossing

Railroad crossing

Lights flash when train is coming.

Railroad crossing

Lights flash and gate goes down when train is coming.

Others are for trains and their workers.

Passenger train

30 / 15

Freight train

Speed limit sign

STATION 1 MILE

Station warning sign

Color light Signal

Stop

Proceed with caution

Go

Semaphores

Stop

Proceed with caution

Go

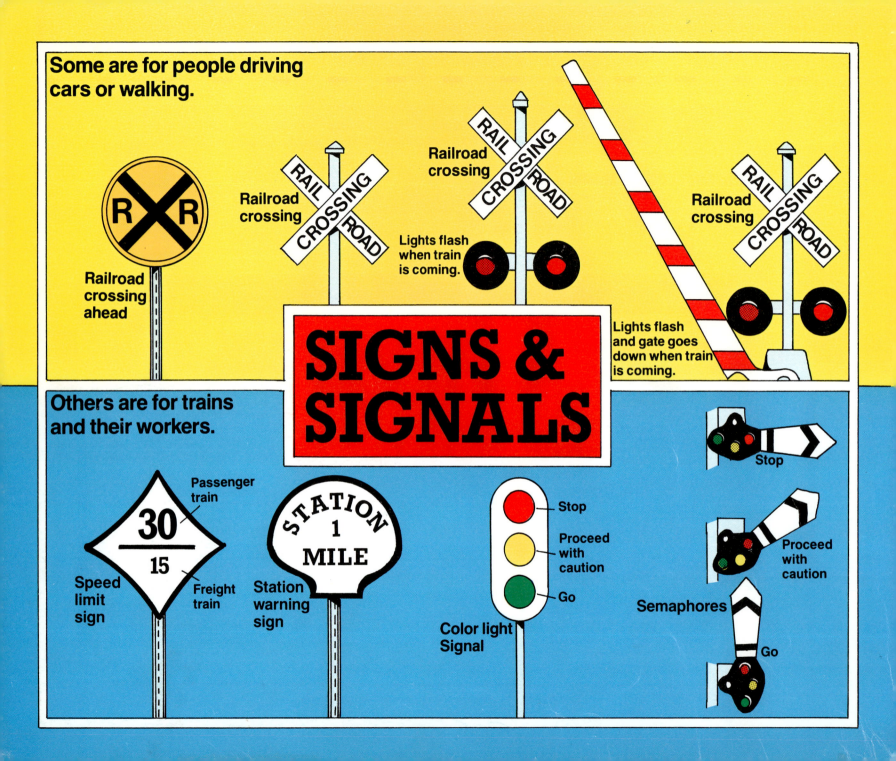